To Barry
With our thanks
from the members of Easter Ross
Christian Concern.

TONY

D1342427

Tony Tindall

TONY

– A Channel of Your Peace –

by Vivienne Wood

This is the story of Tony Tindall as told by him to Vivienne Wood.

MAYFLOWER CHRISTIAN BOOKS

The Publishing Branch of
MAYFLOWER CHRISTIAN BOOKSHOPS CHARITABLE TRUST
114 Spring Road, Sholing, Southampton, Hants.

Copyright © 1988 by Mayflower Christian Books, Southampton

First Published 1988

ISBN 0 907821 05 7

All rights reserved. No part of this publication may be reproduced, stored
in a retrieval system, or transmitted in any form or by any
means—electronic, mechanical, photocopy, recording, or
otherwise—without the prior permission of the copyright owner.

Frontispiece and photographs on pages 65 and 83 are reproduced by kind
permission of The Yorkshire Evening Post.
Other photographs have been supplied by Tony's family and friends.

Line illustrations by Mike Moore.

All Scripture quotations are taken from the New King James Version of
the Bible except on pages 59 and 93 where the New International Version
was required by the author.

Designed and edited by Anne Fountain

Typeset into POSTSCRIPT by Mayflower Christian Books in 12/14 Souvenir
POSTSCRIPT runout by Windsorgraphics, Ringwood, Hampshire
Printed by Itchen Printers Ltd., Southampton

To
Mum and Dad
from Tony

Contents

Acknowledgements

When I met Tony for the first time in June 1987, it was like meeting an old friend for, having heard of his situation we had long prayed for him. As I heard his story from his own lips a conviction grew that it should be written down. Thus developed an association with a young man who was to have a profound influence upon my life; as he did on all with whom he came into contact. Tony was always completely unaware of the effect he had on people; daily the Lord used him to challenge both believers and non-believers alike and my prayer is that this book will continue the testimony he so faithfully and clearly proclaimed while he was alive.

I could not have written this book without the support and encouragement of my husband, Gordon and children, Elizabeth and John. I am indebted to the prayerful interest of various friends, in particular, Janet Grosvenor and Margaret McNabb who read this manuscript in its early stages and urged me to continue. The practical support of friends in Leeds made it possible for me to continue with the writing and re-writing of the script. My dear friend Micheline

Harrison frequently allowed me to use her home for the purpose of interviewing Tony and, in my absence, Debbie Habzidabeh spent many hours with him going over the script until he was happy that it was a faithful record of the Lord's dealings with him.

It has been humbling to be in the will of the Lord, to feel constantly the prayers and support of God's people, and to have known Tony Tindall.

Vivienne Wood, 15th July 1988

Tony's Preface

February 1988

I have been working on this manuscript for a few months now in the sincere hope that it will enable all those who read it to face what life has in store for them, although their situation may be different from mine. Each day is a precious gift from God and whether we are ill or healthy we must value each day and use it to its best advantage; as each new day is given to me and my family, we thank God for further evidences of his goodness to us. My illness has taught me so much; indeed, the quality of my life is richer than it has ever been before: such deep contentment 'passes understanding', and comes through learning to accept the will of God in the sweet reassurance that 'He does all things well'.

Those closest to me have suffered a great deal and together we have learnt what it means to be patient and understanding with each other, to have a positive attitude and a sense of humour during the times of greatest stress. My hope is that they, and others who face losing a loved one, will come to understand what is felt by a victim of disease. Furthermore, I am convinced that many people go through their whole lives and never put right the hurts and frictions that come to most families. It is a tribute to my parents that not only have they given me a very secure childhood, but they have been wonderfully supportive during my illness, even during the times when I have been irritable and self-ish. They have been devastated by the diagnosis—and the prognosis—but I long to show them that what is potentially a disaster for an individual can be turned into a means of grace for God's people. I firmly believe the apostle Paul's words, 'We know that all things work together for good to them that love God, to them who are the called according to his purpose.' (Rom 8:28.)

For that reason I write this book, to help and comfort my mother and father at the present time, to show them and my sister, Louise, and all my family, friends and neighbours, my appreciation and gratitude for all their love and support.

Above all, I write this book to challenge those who read it to consider where they are going in this life and to realise how desperately we all need a Saviour in these days. My prayer is that the Lord Jesus Christ may be glorified and that his kingdom may be extended here on earth.

Tony Tindall

Shadows

Until I was nineteen years old I led an extremely active life, but one without consideration for the things of God, although my father is a devout Roman Catholic and both my sister, Louise, and I were brought up as Catholics. I was born on 2nd January 1967 in Harehills, Leeds and we moved to Woodlesford outside Leeds when I was 5 years old. We had a happy family life together and as children were conscious of having a very caring mother and father who gave us all we needed, but at the same time never spoilt us. My father, who loves every kind of sport, was rather disappointed that I preferred staying inside with my model aeroplanes and toy soldiers to kicking a ball outside with other boys; but I was a solitary child who was completely self-contained within an imaginary, yet intensely vivid world.

Wasted Years

This life-style changed dramatically at secondary school when I joined a gang who were obsessed with 'Heavy Metal' pop music. From the age of fourteen onwards I was never

I was never at home

at home, but spent my time with these friends, wearing de-
nims, a leather jacket, long hair, and experimenting with
alcohol and drugs. I am ashamed to say that I selfishly

neglected my family and refused to spend any time with them. Even my friends stayed in with their families more than I did, and when those friends were unavailable I would find others for company. My parents wanted us to go on family outings and have holidays together, and to this end bought a boat and a caravan, but although I loved my family I did not want them: I wanted my friends instead. It seems to me that it has taken a life-threatening illness for me to realise how much I owe my parents and how deep are the bonds between us. How I thank God that we are closer now than we have ever been as a family and, inevitably, I regret those wasted years.

When I left school at sixteen, my life-style deteriorated further, for I looked older than my years and therefore I was frequently to be found in pubs and night-clubs and—I discovered girls! My first employment was through a Y.T.S. scheme at Tape-Recorder Services which gave me a training in electronics. However, my overspending at the pub quickly ran up large debts and I looked around for an evening job that would supplement my rather meagre Y.T.S. allowance and enable me to repay my debts. Thus began my career as a barman and doorman at Tiffany's Night Club in Leeds which involved extremely long hours; I never came in before 3 a.m. but I had to be up for work the following morning by 7 a.m. Into this hectic life I fitted in a passion for Karate, Akido and my girlfriend. This went on for almost a year and even when a dull ache in my back started around the October of 1985, I carried on with both jobs and hardly had time to notice it.

In December, I moved to a finance company for a higher salary. The work was extremely monotonous; I had to sit at a computer VDU all day and assess people's accounts. I obviously thought the increased salary was worth the

a passion for Karate...

extreme tedium of the job but it was while I was sitting in
one position for long periods of time that I began to notice
a persistent nagging pain in my back. I started to take
paracetamol tablets to ease it. But the pain would not go
away. I continued to work at Tiffany's from choice; the
night-club scene was part of my life and by then it was much
more comfortable for me to stand than to sit down; but my
work at the office proved increasingly stressful. There were
times when I was forced to slouch right under the desk to

operate my VDU because it was so painful to sit in an up-right position. I lived in fear of being fired at work for what must have appeared a slovenly attitude. There were times in the pub when I was having a drink with my friends that they used to tease me about my back and I certainly began to think that my pain threshold must be very low.

Back trouble

I commented to my family as we sat down to an evening meal one night that my back was giving me a lot of trouble. Occasionally my father has back trouble from sciatica so we all came to the conclusion that it must be a bad bout of sciatica and I was advised by a physiotherapist to try exercises to ease it. One exercise had me hanging from the garage door! Still the pain refused to go away. We thought I might have a slipped disc; there was by this time a small lump at the base of my pelvis, so I decided to go to my father's osteopath for manipulation and massage. Each time I visited the osteopath he was convinced the lump was getting smaller. As he manipulated my back I kept hearing clicks: "D'you hear that click?" he said, "That's your disc going back in." On reflection now it was obvious that something more serious was going on but at that time it was the furthest thought from our minds.

Has the pain gone?

At Tiffany's one night, I broke a bone in my little finger. In the casualty department at Leeds General Infirmary, while they were x-raying my finger, I mentioned to the radiographer that my back was persistently troubling me. She agreed to x-ray my pelvis and gave me the result immediately: the x-ray film revealed nothing wrong at all and I went home totally reassured.

But I was still in constant pain. Desperately I tried to put it out of my mind, to rationalise it, to overcome it, to relax and forget about it. Each day I would wake up and my first thought would be, "Has the pain gone?" It never had.

I kept going to my doctor who gave me some anti-inflammatory tablets and finally referred me to the hospital for more x-rays which, once again, proved clear. Only once did I entertain the thought for a few minutes that it might be something sinister but then dismissed the idea as being entirely ludicrous. I had read a story in the paper about a man who had had back pain for months and one day collapsed and died. The post-mortem had revealed cancer in his spine. I remember thinking, "I wonder if I've got that?" and then immediately saying to myself, "It can't be! It's impossible".

Early in February the pain intensified and there were times when I felt I could not endure it any more. One night I could not sleep at all and I paced up and down my room in agony. I did not want to wake my parents up so I spent the entire night wandering around my room, crying. How well I know King David's feelings as he writes in the book of Psalms:
O Lord, heal me, for my bones are troubled...
I am weary with my groaning;
All night I make my bed swim;
I drench my couch with my tears.   (Psalm 6:2,6.)

In the early hours of the morning my mother woke and heard a sound like the moaning of a kitten. She rushed into my room and was dismayed to find me in such overwhelming pain. She ran downstairs and fetched the anti-inflammatory tablets which the doctor had given me. They had never worked before but this time they took the pain away.

Such sweet relief! For the first time in months I was without pain. It was an extraordinary feeling of freedom.

My mother insisted that I went straight to the hospital casualty for further advice and investigations. It was a cold and snowy day and the brilliant sunshine reflected and intensified the glistening frost as I walked into St. James's Hospital Casualty Department. The tablets were wearing off, I was desperate for some relief, yet my further attempts at penetrating the medical world were thwarted as they turned me away:
"We are sorry; there is nothing we can do for you. Back pain is so common and you must come to us through your family doctor."

"Surely you can check me?" I asked.
"There's nothing wrong," said the doctor, as he felt my back in an effort to placate me, "now you must return to work and come back to us through your own doctor."
I tried to explain to him that I was not trying to avoid work—rather it was an acute problem that I could not endure much longer; he was just not interested. Such an attitude seemed common, perhaps because some people use back pain as an excuse to avoid work. I returned to work that morning feeling very low and the pain seemed to return with a vengeance. I could hardly bear to work at my VDU and was aware that my supervisor kept looking at me; I knew that my days with the company were numbered.

At Last!

I reluctantly returned to my own doctor who continued to refuse me stronger pain-killers but who did, once more, refer me to the hospital for x-rays. Yet again, these proved completely clear and the doctors were puzzled by the continuing mystery of my pain. They thought it must be a trapped nerve that could not be picked up on an x-ray. At the end of March 1986, I went to Pinderfields Hospital in Wakefield for further x-rays but whichever hospital I went to, the result was always the same.

The inevitable event happened on Friday, April 9th—I was sacked. I was devastated at the time but realise now that God's hand was upon the situation even then. If I had not been fired, then I would have forced myself to carry on working. As it happened, losing my job brought things to a climax. The following Monday I went to the doctor's for the result of the latest x-rays. Urged on by my parents, I insisted on something being done about my back pain which had gone on for long enough. Reluctantly, he wrote to the specialist asking for my name to be included on the two month waiting-list for admission to hospital for investigation of back pain. At last!

The next day a friend called around to see me and asked me if I would like to go swimming with him. Normally I hate swimming and nothing will induce me to go to the public swimming baths, but for some reason I agreed to go with him. After all, swimming sometimes relieves back pain and I was desperate for any relief. There in the water I was free from pain. It was exhilarating! I resolved to go swimming regularly as this obviously alleviated the muscle strain in my back. However, just as I had felt an intoxicating feeling of freedom from pain in the water, when I emerged from the pool, waves of pain once more swept over me in increasing ferocity. I shall never know how I managed to get home but once there, I collapsed under their savage attack. My mother was at home but my father was at work and there was no-one around to take me to hospital. In the providence of God, my father rang up just at that moment, and my mother was able to tell him how bad I was. He came home immediately and soon we were heading towards St. James's Hospital. Once in Casualty, the doctors soon realised that I was not deluding myself or trying to fool them and they became convinced that there was something in my back that they could not see. As usual, further x-rays revealed nothing, but for the first time I was taken seriously and that night they admitted me to the Orthopaedic ward for more intensive tests.

Dark Days

You might imagine that I lay in my bed that first night in a strange ward full of fear and apprehension. You would be mistaken! I merely thought, "This is going to be great—two weeks' holiday. I've put my disc out and I shall be given traction for a couple of weeks and be waited on by pretty nurses." I was determined to enjoy it. I was in a modern, six-bedded ward directly opposite a man with his neck in traction. We started talking to each other and carried on talking most of the night—even when others in the ward kept telling us to be quiet. His name was Bob Johns; he was a policeman, the local Accident Prevention Officer. We established a rapport immediately; I felt at home with him and loved to talk with him and hear his soft Devonian accent. A firm friendship was struck up that night as we compared experiences and swapped stories.

During the following days, I was subjected to many x-rays and intensive tests. I continued to enjoy myself however, relishing all the attention from the medical staff during the day, and visits from numerous friends in the evenings. For reasons I cannot understand even now, I behaved

Bob Johns

appallingly to my parents, virtually ignoring them when they came to visit me. I loved being surrounded by my friends and had no time for my family. They describe the many nights when they could not get near me in my bed because of the number of friends crowding around, and they would just sit in the waiting room or slip away. Bob Johns tried to tell me that it is always your parents who stick by you in the end when all your friends have left you alone but I was too short-sighted and selfish to take any notice of his words. I will never know how much I hurt my parents during those early days nor could I have comprehended how prophetic his words would be.

The Truth

Then our peace was shattered. A further series of detailed x-rays had revealed a small spot which they would investigate further by a C.A.T. body scan. We were told that the doctors suspected that there was a tumour in the pelvis but that they needed further investigations to discover whether it was benign or malignant. Malign, benign? These words meant nothing to me and for the next few days I plied people, especially Bob, with questions concerning the nature of tumours, and, inevitably, cancer itself. I realised that it sounded sinister and we all grew desperate to know the truth. After the C.A.T. scan and a bone scan I told the doctor that I was ready for the truth and wanted to be told at the same time as my family or, indeed, before them. I wanted to avoid the situation whereby my family was withholding information from me; I could not bear the sort of deception that illness sometimes forces on families.

While we waited for the results of those tests, my parents were agonising over whether they should go on their holiday to Portugal. My father had booked a week's golfing there and my mother and sister were to join him a week later. We all urged him to go and very reluctantly he agreed, providing we kept in daily contact with him by telephone. My mother and sister kept coming in to see me and, increasingly, we felt as if a dark shadow was hanging over all of us as we waited for the results. But nothing could have prepared us for what we were going to hear.

One evening, at about 6 p.m., Mr. Lawton, the orthopaedic surgeon, came into the ward and sat on my bed. He brought out all the scans, x-rays and results and spread them

over my bed. He slowly showed me the films one by one. There before my eyes I saw white blotches all over the x-ray of my lungs. On the scan, I saw a large, oval shape which went through the pelvis bone and pushed the skin out on the other side, which explained the swelling on my back. This was the cause of all the trouble: a vicious malignant tumour which had rapidly spread to other parts of my body. It had obviously been left far too long but apparently it is very difficult to distinguish soft tissue masses on ordinary x-rays. Mr. Lawton stayed with me for about twenty minutes and tried to make the best of it: "I don't know what the chances are of getting rid of it," he said, "It looks very serious but we'll try our best. You'll have to go to Cookridge Hospital for treatment. We hope to shrink it down so that we can operate on it eventually. We'll do all we can to help you."

I was speechless. I cannot describe the shock, the bewilderment, the lostness. In vain I tried to gather my thoughts together to ask some questions but the words stuck in my throat. When Mr. Lawton saw my mother and sister coming down the ward, crying, he left us together. Unknown to me he had already spoken to them in the sister's office; my mother described how Mr. Lawton had called them both in, and the ward sister had followed with a tray of tea. It was then that my mother knew that it was bad news; the tea was a compassionate gesture amidst the hopelessness.

Mr. Lawton had told them everything. My mother obviously realised the implications of what he was telling them, but I did not begin to comprehend them. I tried to comfort and reassure them:
"Don't worry!" I said, "Look, it's going to be O.K. We'll get through this; they'll get rid of it. They'll just get rid of it. Everything's going to be all right."
I just assumed that the doctors would be able to find a cure. I was so naïve about cancer but my mother suspected how serious it really was. They were absolutely devastated and wanted to stay with me all night but I comforted them and reassured them again and again that everything would be all right. I finally suggested they went home, telephoned my father and tried to get some sleep.

After they had left, I slowly walked up and down the ward, trying to absorb the implications of what we had been told. I stopped to look out of the large window at the bottom of the ward; it was a dark, wintry night and I could see people in a nearby brightly-lit church hall doing Judo. I could not stop the tears coming to my eyes as I recalled how I used to do Akido before the onset of pain. It seemed a long time ago and I felt so old that night. The thought of throwing my body about now was unthinkable; it even hurt me to kick a ball. I kept saying over and over to myself, "I've got cancer," but that did not seem real to me: it would not sink in. It was truly like a bad dream from which I hoped I would wake up one day. Tears ran down my face as I saw myself as others would see me, faced with cancer and the prospect of dying. The only poor consolation was that the mystery of the pain had been solved and doctors and friends need speculate no more. Tears of fear, as well as relief and hope at the prospect of some positive treatment, ran down my cheeks that night as I contemplated issues too great for me to comprehend or handle on my own.

Tense Weeks

The next two weeks were tense. Mum and Louise had telephoned my father who, understandably, was distraught. His first reaction was to come straight home. We persuaded him to stay and the nurses and doctors joined me in urging my mother to join him for the remainder of their holiday. Very reluctantly she went, agreeing that it was better for her to have a break at this stage of the illness while I was occupied having more tests at St. James's. She agreed to go, on condition that they promised not to go ahead with any treatment, such as chemotherapy, until she returned. Mr. Lawton gave her his word that I would not be given any specific treatment, apart from pain control, until she was there to be consulted and involved.

The doctors' first priority was indeed to sort out my pain control and when they finally gave me 120 mg of morphine daily in tablet form, I was ecstatic with the relief from pain. Anyone who has known the feeling when continuous pain is abated will appreciate my euphoria. It reminded me of the experience in the swimming baths when all my pain seemed to be washed away.

At every stage the doctors informed me what the tests were revealing. They were honest and direct with me: I wanted it that way. The C.A.T. scan had revealed white cancerous blotches all over my lungs; the painful bone marrow test which I had had at Cookridge Hospital also proved positive and they gave me more information about the tumour on my pelvis which is known as a Ewings sarcoma. It is more usually a children's disease and rarely found in the pelvis. It is also one of the fastest growing tumours. The remaining worry was that it had spread to my liver but in fact this proved to be a groundless fear: the unusual shape of my liver turned out to be a variation of normal which had temporarily confused the specialists.

After my family had returned from holiday I was transferred to Cookridge Hospital under the capable management of Dr. Sheila Cartwright, returning to St. James's Hospital for periods of convalescence. When we asked her what my chances were, she informed me that I had a 10% chance of the treatment being a success but she was going to employ a powerful new drug in a course of chemotherapy using the most toxic dose that could be given. It was in fact a tribute to my youth, my relative fitness, stamina and strength that I was able to tolerate the massive toxicity of such drugs.

The only alternative would be a radical 'hind-quarter' operation which would remove my leg and thigh: however, surgeons at St. James's would not entertain such a drastic measure. She further told us that if the disease had been left unchecked for a further two months, it would have been too late for the doctors to do anything. God's timing was perfect for my spiritual pilgrimage.

Within a few days I was being prepared for the course of chemotherapy, though nothing could have adequately prepared me for this experience. It seemed to me like entering hell itself; the 'weeping and gnashing of teeth' describe well a human's response to this particular isolation and agony. The sickness was overwhelming. I seemed to lose everything: my memory, my consciousness, my hair, my appetite, my body weight, and gained in return: mouth ulcers, sickness, boils, constipation and the most irritating hiccoughs. I longed for the treatment to finish but can honestly say that I never wanted to die. Through it all my iron will to live was as strong as ever.

In moments of lucidity, I realised I was on a ward with older, dying people and that depressed me deeply. At my request I was moved to a 'younger' ward but I later appreciated the wisdom of the nursing staff's first decision, for the contrast was too painful for me. I was in fact more at home with the 'chronically' sick, so they understood when I asked to be returned to my former ward. Such treatment affects different people in different ways; there are varying degrees of chemotherapy and there were many patients who were on lower doses than myself who could laugh, talk and eat whilst being treated. Clearly, I had no place with them at that time. Such is the resilience of the human frame that the later phases of chemotherapy were never to affect me in the same way as that first course.

It was during a period of convalescence in St. James's Hospital, after a course of treatment, that I received a mysterious parcel, securely bound and anonymously marked: "from someone who loves you." I was intrigued. I opened

it up to find a book entitled *The Happiest People on Earth*.
It was to prove a turning point in my life.

3
Hope

I waited until visiting time that evening to ask my friends if they knew anything about the book. I was curious to find out who it was from because I had been absolutely thrilled and amazed as I had read it, and I secretly hoped it was from my ex-girlfriend. If only the claims in the book were true... No-one owned up to it, but night after night, as my friends crowded around my bed, I pursued the matter with them. They began to see how important it was to me and finally one of them told my mother who had sent the book. They had not wanted to tell me for fear of disappointing me—I had really loved my girlfriend and sadly it was not from her. Instead, it was from a girl, whom I scarcely knew, at the company where I worked. My friends arranged for Lorraine and her boyfriend, Nick, to come along to the hospital one evening to meet my parents who were as anxious to meet them as I was.

Lorraine and Nick came in and met my parents outside the ward in the smoking area. They talked with them about the possibilities of divine healing, which was the subject of the book they had sent me, and recounted numerous stories of people they knew who had had hands laid on them and had been healed. Nothing seemed to be too hard for God: arthritis, cancer, orthopaedic injuries, depression and psychiatric illnesses were cured as well as everyday ailments. Indeed so positive were they that they believed no Christian need ever be sick. My father was nearly overwhelmed with joy as he listened to their gospel and my mother will never forget the impression Lorraine made on her; her face was like an angel's as she spoke of God's willingness to heal his children. Indeed so responsive were my parents that Nick and Lorraine prayed with them before they came onto the ward to meet me.

I will never forget the look on my father's face as he came into the ward and introduced them both to me. Like my father, I was receptive to anything and eagerly listened to Nick as he began to talk with me about healing. He was a good talker; he was so confident and self-assured. He thrust Scripture at me so convincingly that I was amazed at his knowledge and found it very difficult to argue with him. At the end of visiting time, Lorraine said, "D'you mind if I pray with you?" I could not believe it. Nick was only about thirty-four years old and Lorraine in her twenties—such young people—and yet already they were on this personal level with God. They had such authority. I could not believe that there were people, other than priests, who could have a personal relationship with God. Surely only priests and nuns prayed with you and addressed God so intimately?

I can hardly describe the new joy and hope my family and I were filled with that night. These two people had given us such hope at a time when we needed it the most. I had been told that I must rest and had not been out of bed for a fortnight. That night I defied orders, got out of bed and actually jumped about! My heart was overflowing with such optimism and faith. I had always believed in God and assumed I was a Christian. After all, I had devoutly attended Mass in my younger days and my best subject at school was R.E.—this healing was obviously mine for the asking.

Nick sent me another book and on my next leave from hospital, my father and I were able to go with them to their breakfast healing meeting in Bradford. It was a wonderful meeting; we had never attended anything like it before. It must have lasted for over three hours but the time seemed to go so quickly. We particularly enjoyed the beautiful songs of worship and fellowship that stirred our hearts. Many people prayed and shared their testimonies of how God had touched their lives.

the force inside my head

The speaker asked those who were ill to go to the front; my father came forward with me and the speaker asked me the nature of my illness. He began praying over me in

English and then swiftly moved into a curious language
which I had learnt from the book was known as 'speaking
in tongues'. To me it sounded incomprehensible but they
assured me it was a 'heavenly' language. He put his hands
on my head and I experienced a feeling like a vacuum
cleaner sucking all the air out of my chest. Then from my
toes upward, I felt as if something was being poured in slowly, right up to my head. Like others around me I started to
fall backwards on the floor; the psychological pressure was
extremely powerful and as the force inside my head started
to push me backwards, I gladly gave in to it. I fell down on
my back; my laughter was mixed with crying, and tears of
joy and relief poured down my cheeks. We were deeply
moved by it all. Nick came across to me and said, "Now
you're healed, brother, do you want to be baptised in the
Spirit?" I did not understand what he meant but I did not
want to offend him and besides, the feeling was so marvellous, I wanted everything going! With his hands placed on
my head, Nick said, "You have now received the Holy
Spirit. You have been born again. You are a new person—
how do you feel?" I felt wonderful—euphoric and ecstatic
and certainly, there was no pain. With his arms around us
both, Nick looked at my father and said, "Dad, meet new
son," and turning to me, "Son, meet new dad."

Nick and I walked out into the morning sunshine. We
strolled together by the swimming pool in the beautiful
grounds of the hotel where the meetings were held. I felt
so well and was convinced that I had been healed. My father
walked across the lawns to meet us; he had stayed behind
to receive further ministry. Nick walked between us sharing
details of a prophecy God had given him concerning me. It
took the form of a dream: he had seen a hand going up-
wards holding a mummified body whose bandages were
being removed. Under the rotting bandages, a revitalised

It took the form of a dream

person emerged, healed and renewed. The Lord had revealed to Nick that I would be healed and that my testimony
would bring thousands of people to himself. Furthermore it

was imperative that my own father should lay hands on me to complete the healing.

After the 'prayer-breakfast' I longed to tell everybody of my healing. My father and I quickly returned home to share this new hope with my mother. She was amazed as she listened to all we had to tell her. Slowly, hope filled her heart too and as a family we were closer than we had ever been before.

I was eager to return to St. James's to tell them all about my experiences. I sincerely believed that the cancer had gone and that there would be no need for further chemotherapy; it would only take an x-ray to prove to the medical staff that I was healed. The doctors and nurses listened sympathetically but nobody knew what to say when the new x-ray showed that there was no improvement. I made them get out the old x-rays to compare them, but to my profound dismay, I realised the white blotches on my lungs were still clearly visible.

Later that week when I returned to Cookridge for further chemotherapy, I wrote to Dr. Cartwright while I was waiting on the ward:

'Dear Dr. Cartwright,

I am a Catholic and go to church so I do believe in God. Whilst I was at St. James's Hospital a book was sent to me called 'The Happiest People On Earth', with a little note saying, "from someone who loves you". I had no idea who it was from, but my

mum found out that it was from a girl I used to work
with, so she asked Lorraine and her boyfriend to come
and see us. We had all read the book and found it
very interesting. In the book were accounts of healings
and prophecies. If you don't believe in God at all or
are not sure, you won't believe the book. But I do and
did.

Nick and Lorraine came to see me and explained
more about it—about God and Christianity. They're
not religious fanatics or anything, just good Christians
who want to help. They gave me another highly ac-
claimed book to read called, 'The Holy Spirit and
You'. Everything said in this book is backed up by the
Holy Bible; verses such as: 'For I am the Lord who
heals you' (Ex 15:26), and 'I will take sickness away
from the midst of you.' (Ex 23:25.) I read all this and
talked it over with Nick and Lorraine and—I admit—it
does seem very hard to believe. However, one Saturday whilst I was at home, I was invited to go to one of
their meetings in Bradford. My father and I went with
them and were very impressed. I have never seen so
many happy people together. There were doctors, di-
rectors, managers... many very influential and intelli-
gent men. People stood up to give their testimonies,
to tell their own stories of why they had turned to
God. Some of them had been miraculously healed—
one gave an account of a short leg that had grown
longer; another of arthritis that was instantly cured.

Nick revealed his gift of prophecy to us by a remarkable story. While he was in America, he had attended a meeting where a man in front of him told
the church that he was riddled with cancer and the
doctors could do nothing for him. After he told
everyone, they all prayed for him. As if he were day-

dreaming, Nick saw a hand, like a claw, tear out of the man's back and the wound healed up straight away. He shared this prophecy with the group. The man met Nick later at another meeting and told him that he had been to hospital for tests; the medical staff thought he must have a twin brother because further tests showed there was nothing at all wrong with him: he was completely cured.

At the end of the meeting in Bradford they asked if there was anyone there who wanted to come forward for ministry. I went forward and told the speaker I had cancer. He put his hands on my head and prayed for God to heal me. Then I started to go backwards. I tried to hold myself up but I kept falling until I was lying on the floor. I tried to pick myself up but it felt as if I weighed a ton—I just couldn't move. Then I was told that I was healed.

Something really has happened... the swelling on my back has gone down... I believe that I no longer have cancer in my lungs. Something very important did happen although you may not believe it. If I am not cured then fair enough. But I am.

> *Yours sincerely,*
> *Anthony Tindall.'*

Dr. Cartwright told me later that she was moved by the letter but could not deny the evidence of the x-rays, so she filed this letter away in my notes. Further x-rays at Cookridge confirmed what St. James's had said—that there was no change. I was bewildered and confused but when I returned to my friends in Bradford, they assured me this was quite normal: God's timing is perfect and he works in mysterious and unorthodox ways to confound man and to demonstrate his power. "Don't worry!" they said, "You are going to get better: Father has told us." I was so new to this idea of talking to God and about God as a father, and was open to the Lord for whatever he had to give us or ask us to do. However, my ignorance was profound; I did not know how to test situations by the Scriptures nor man's claims by the Word of God.

A few mornings later I woke up to find my father leaning over me with his hands on my back to fulfil Nick's prophecy. He had been too embarrassed to do it when I was awake, but I loved him for this demonstration of his love and faith and, indeed, all the other ways my parents continually showed their support and concern for me.

Peace With God

As the weeks went by I was no better. In July we all travelled to a Catholic church in Tadcaster, a town between Leeds and York, to attend a healing Mass administered by a leading Catholic healer. The church was packed long before the service began. It was an emotional and moving service with lots of singing and holding up hands in praise to God. Many healings, both physical and spiritual, were claimed through the name of Jesus. After the service a few of the more seriously ill from the congregation went into the garden at the back of the church where the healer laid hands on us all, one by one, and prayed for our healing. We all sat down on some chairs in a circle and then he turned to me:
"You know that God can heal you?"
"Yes, I know he can," I replied with feeling.
"You know you're going to get better?" He hugged me twice. "D'you feel the warmth coming through?"
"Yes," I answered.

He seemed very taken with me:
"This lad is going to get married," he pronounced, "this is a lad with faith. He's not going to die; in fact, you may invite

me to his wedding!"
My mother was thrilled and we all took it as a sure promise
for the future.

On another occasion I went to a week-end Healing Conference in Scarborough where once more I experienced a
new belief in the power of healing. I sat by myself in the
hall one afternoon and a lady came up behind me and put
her hands on my shoulders and told me that she had received a powerful feeling compelling her to tell me that I
was very special to God, that he loved me and would heal
me. She was a complete stranger and said that she had
never had such a feeling before and it was totally out of
character for her to do such a thing. I returned home to tell
my parents all that had happened over the week-end and
we were all renewed with a fresh optimism that I would be
healed.

Another time we went to a fellowship in Haworth where
a doctor was preaching. Hands were laid on me, and they
claimed a demon was cast out. It was there that I slowly
began to realise that when healers laid hands on you they
sometimes pressed down quite hard to force you to fall and
thus give the impression that a mighty power was at work.
It was almost impossible to resist such pressure because of
the intensely emotional and psychological atmosphere that
was always present on these occasions. I was beginning to
question all the procedures but I was desperate to be healed
and besides, I did not then have the knowledge of the Scriptures nor the confidence to challenge those who proclaimed
healing. I wanted them to be right—so very much.

For many weeks we sustained the charade that I had been
healed. When I was in agony, Nick would say to me, "How
can this be? You've got to have faith, Tony. Stop taking the

pain-killers and prove God. You have to believe that you have been healed and learn to accept this gift from God. If you don't, you are in danger of losing it; God will take the healing away from you. You must act as if you are completely whole and throw away the medication." He would strengthen his position further with stories about people who had demonstrated sufficient faith and had been healed.

When I expressed unbelief and scepticism about my own 'healing', he introduced the concept of various blockages, or besetting sins, that might be preventing my healing. Such introspective teaching caused me to consider my past and present sins as potential obstacles to the healing of my body. Although I consider such teaching to be erroneous now, I do believe that God used Nick's words to cause me to think deeply about my life and Christ's demands for his followers. Because I had been brought up to go to church and had regularly attended Mass I assumed I was a Christian, but although I was accustomed to the priests granting absolution, I knew nothing of forgiveness of sins by a personal Saviour, or the need for a holy walk with God. How gracious is our heavenly father who 'accepts us in the Beloved' even when we are seeking him with impure and selfish motives. God, in his mercy, had a plan for me laid out, 'before the foundation of the world, that [I] should be holy and without blame before him in love' (Eph 1:4.) Gradually I began to realise that my greatest need was not for a physical healing which would only provide temporary relief, but for a new heart. I needed, as the Bible puts it, 'to be born again'. Out of such soul-searching and dissatisfaction with my life were sown the seeds of repentance and faith.

Urged on by Nick, I looked earnestly within my life to discover the 'blocking factors' that were preventing my healing. The first thing to go was my collection of Rock records.

Nick had a huge bonfire in his garden one day and I threw on all my Ozzie Osbourne and Black Sabbath records while Nick and his friend chanted repeatedly "In Jesus's name".

There were a number of books in our house by a famous medium which I insensitively tackled my mother about one day. "The reason I'm not getting better is you, mum," I accused and insisted she got rid of them all. She was heartbroken at the implication that she was the reason for the failure of the healing.

Getting drunk had been a way of life for me for three years and for a long time I could not see what was wrong with it. Gradually, the pleasure I had in going to the pub and wild parties began to abate and I grew increasingly dissatisfied with that way of life. The Holy Spirit was truly working in my life, for no-one, left to himself, chooses the path of righteousness. Instead of going to the pub, I began to prefer to stay in and read the Bible. I read it eagerly, gradually becoming more and more convinced that my spiritual need was greater than my physical need. The words 'What shall it profit a man if he gain the whole world and lose his own soul?' (Mark 8:36) kept going round and round in my mind.

The turning point in my life came when I went to a wild party at Christmas and got horribly drunk. As the alcohol wore off in the early hours of the morning, I came to my senses, like the prodigal son, and was deeply convicted of my sins. I thought that if I was supposed to be a Christian, what sort of a witness was my life to people? I dreaded someone challenging me about it. I realised in my heart of hearts that I was not a Christian. That night I confessed my sins to God, admitting my hopeless state before him. I looked into my own heart and saw its dark and iniquitous guile and then I looked to Jesus and saw his glory and holiness. The gulf between us seemed greater than ever and yet I read in his Word, 'If we confess our sins, he is faithful and just to forgive us our sins, and to cleanse us from all unrighteousness.' (1 John 1:9.) I took the Lord at his word and, confessing my desperate need for a Saviour, put my trust in him that night and knew the deep peace and joy that Christ alone can bring. I put my life into his hands and trusted him for whatever dark days might lie ahead.

Is he moaning again?

False Prophets

Increasingly I was criticised for my lack of faith which was held to be the reason why I remained unhealed; indeed this is the ultimate 'blockage' for which there is no human answer. The manipulation is devious; the victim is left isolated, with a tremendous sense of failure and guilt when he realises that his faith is not strong enough. The healers are exonerated: they cannot lose.

I cannot forget my last meeting with Nick and Lorraine in their home. Lorraine asked me how I was.
"The scan shows it's still there," I said.
"You don't believe that?" she said, "It's gone—you know it's gone."
"That's ridiculous," I replied, "The big tumour is still there. I can feel it; I know it's there."
Nick walked in and looked at Lorraine. "Is he moaning again?" he asked.
"No, it's not moaning: it's unbelief," she replied.

Nick announced to everyone there: "God's been speaking to me in the car. We're going to try something new."

Turning to me he said: "You've got to pray while the rest of us speak in tongues."
We gathered chairs around and held hands. The lights were turned off and I felt uncomfortable and embarrassed at having to pray aloud.

I stumbled, "Your will not ours, whatever happens..." and faltered.
Lorraine took it up, "Please God, let it be your will, not ours."
Everyone prayed and then Nick spoke as if he were the direct mouthpiece of God: "My precious, precious children, why do you hurt me? How long must it be before you realise your need of me? My only desire is that you will be made whole, that you will turn from your unbelieving ways and put your trust in me. Then I shall lead you into paths of great joy, peace and deliverance..."

He carried on in this way for a while and after the lights went back on, I asked him, "Nick, is that called interpretation of tongues or is it prophecy?" I was still confused by the terms and references they used for their esoteric meetings but I was not prepared for their reactions. Lorraine drew her breath in sharply and looked at Nick. They were deeply offended that I had asked that.

She put her head in her hands and groaned, "Don't you understand that it's God speaking? I am warning you: take heed of what God says."
"I only wanted to know," I replied.
Nick got up. "I have the gift of prophecy and it strikes me that you're jealous of the gifts that other people have. What is your problem? What is wrong with you?"
"I am not convinced that the Holy Spirit works in this way," I answered.
"There is more unbelief in you now than when I first met you," he hissed.
He continued to hurl more abuse at me and then put his hand in his pocket and drew out a fifty pence piece which he placed on the table saying, "That fifty pence piece has more faith and belief in it than you have ever had."
With that he walked out of the room, and I left soon after, puzzled and hurt, but somehow convinced that God would not let me go.

I had completely believed everything I had been told by these friends. Maybe I was naïve, but I did not then have the knowledge of the Scriptures nor the confidence to challenge them. Besides, I was desperate to be healed; these people cannot really lose for they are dealing with desperate people who will believe anything. They are kind, well-meaning Christian people who emphasise certain aspects of their faith but ignore other essential truths. The tragedy of their teaching is that they emphasise the healing of the body and mind, but it was a long time before I was confronted with my need to be born again of the Holy Spirit of God. They tell you that you need inner healing but not inner cleansing. They emphasise wholeness here on earth but fail to prepare you for eternity. At that time I only wanted God for the physical healing he could offer; I had not been confronted with my desperate spiritual need. I know now that had he healed me, I would soon have returned to my old ways and forgotten him. Like my friends, I had been engrossed with the sensational, with the here and now, with the things that are seen, rather than unseen.

God, in his sovereign grace, had used Nick and Lorraine to introduce me to the things of God, and I am truly grateful to them for the many hours they spent with me. As I look back on my association with these Christians, my family and I thank God for the hope they gave us at such a dark and desperate time and for the time they spent with me as together we sought to understand the ways of God to man, but as I came to read the Bible more and more for myself, I learnt to rely less upon them and more upon the Lord. Indeed this independence had been encouraged by Nick over the months, for he was conscious that I relied far too much on him.

Their view of God's dealings with us is, however, flawed, for they assume they can start from a position of strength. They believe that God does not want any of his children to be sick: healing is their right as 'children of the King'. Furthermore, they cheapen God and do not approach him with the awe and reverence he demands. Consequently, they are not conscious of their own shortcomings and weaknesses before a holy God. Their limited view of the Scriptures gives them an unholy confidence before the Throne of Grace. Their arrogance enables them to manipulate people and situations because they say they have the mind of the Lord and who can argue with that?

At times I was aware that the phrase, 'for God's glory' rolled too easily from their tongues, yet in reality, the implications of their teachings brought glory to man and not to God. Some of the leaders could be very arrogant: they used situations to display their knowledge of Scripture and to build up and intensify their authority. Furthermore, the healings I have observed in meetings have sometimes been extremely dubious; the people have only been 'healed' partially, if at all, and the frightening implication is that God— the great creator and sustainer of the universe—cannot do a job properly. These and many other thoughts I mulled over during the early months of 1987 when I was very much alone.

Caring For Life 7

I continued to attend my local Catholic church as I had done throughout my illness, and I had much joy in reading and studying the Bible on my own. I was particularly struck by these verses:

> For we know that the whole creation groans and labours with birth pangs together until now. And not only they, but we also who have the first-fruits of the Spirit, even we ourselves groan within ourselves, waiting for...the redemption of our body.
> (Rom 8:22-23.)

I began to realise that far from running away from pain and suffering, these were the inevitable experiences of a fallen world. Furthermore, in the Scriptures, suffering is frequently linked with the future promise of glory, and the Lord gave me glimpses of my future inheritance when pain and anguish will be no more: 'For I consider that the sufferings of this present time are not worthy to be compared with the glory which shall be revealed in us.' (Rom 8:18.)

These verses were to sustain me through a further period of testing as I returned to hospital for a seven week course of radiotherapy. Like the chemotherapy, I was given the maximum dosage which made me extremely sick. They directed the radiotherapy at my pelvis, which irritated my digestive system. I had never experienced such sickness and vomiting as I had at that time. I was left feeling utterly drained, weak and confused, and thought I would never recover from that treatment to live a normal life again.

Nevertheless, during the next few weeks of convalescence at home, I gradually recovered my strength and interest in life once more and I began to look around for something to do to fill the long days. I was convinced that the Lord still had a work for me to do in this life; I was longing to tell others about my new-found faith and I hoped to find some Christian work to do in this period before my last stage of chemotherapy. I was well enough to be attended at home if need be, by a Macmillan nurse from St. Gemma's Hospice.

Bob Johns, whom I had met in hospital, has a lot of contacts among people involved in charity organizations, so I telephoned him. He promised me that he would look out for something that would give me an interest and be of service to others. The very next day a worker from Leeds Reformed Baptist Church (L.R.B.C.) contacted Bob to introduce him to the recently formed Christian charity, 'Caring for Life', which was run by people from L.R.B.C. They had been given two derelict houses by Leeds City Council which they were renovating to provide homes for destitute young people. Bob immediately 'phoned me, suggesting that this was just the sort of work that would suit me. It did appeal to me so I 'phoned the Rev. Peter Parkinson the next day and arranged for an interview.

A week later I went to see Peter at his farm on the out-skirts of Leeds. We 'clicked' immediately, sharing the same sense of humour—peculiarly Yorkshire some would say—and the same interests and hobbies. Above all, I could re-late to him on a spiritual level; I listened eagerly to things he said and a deep longing stirred in me to study the Bible further for myself.

The first time I went to a service at L.R.B.C., Peter spoke on Paul's 'thorn in the flesh'. I had already studied these verses for myself and was thrilled as I heard them ex-pounded. The pastor's understanding of them was similar

The first time I went to L.R.B.C.

to mine, that God allows suffering to bring us to the point of complete dependence upon him. Our faith is sharpened and we find that his grace is sufficient for us. This interpre-tation was so radically different from the one held by the Christians who had influenced me up until then. Many of them had expected—and demanded—God to eliminate suffering from their lives. They preached prosperity and physical wholeness ignoring the spiritual benefits that suffering can bring to the believer.

> When through fiery trials thy pathway shall lie,
> His grace all-sufficient shall be thy supply;
> The flame shall not hurt thee, His only design
> Thy dross to consume and thy gold to refine.

> The soul that on Jesus has leaned for repose
> He will not, He cannot, desert to its foes;
> That soul, though all hell should endeavour to shake,
> He never will leave, He will never forsake.

The second Sunday left me thinking deeply; Peter expounded 2 Corinthians 12:11-12 and this time I disagreed with him. The months of indoctrination had penetrated deeply and I thought he was very wrong, but such conflicts were very good for me: they forced me to go away and study the Bible. Eagerly I read every commentary and sermon I could find on that passage and soon that hunger extended to other parts of Scripture. To catch up for the lost years I soaked up the Scriptures which are indeed 'able to make you wise unto salvation.'

It was February 1987 when I first met Peter; I was still having chemotherapy but by the end of April I had finished my course of treatment. To be able to visit friends in the church, do evangelistic work and help Peter with 'Caring for Life', gave me some of the happiest times of my life. I was able to drive myself around Leeds and exercise a ministry in the church. Peter's vision was to provide homes for young people after they left Social Services community homes. The way the Lord had given Peter, many years ago, the vision to 'care for life' for many of these deprived and rejected young people, and the Lord's faithfulness and provision in establishing the vision, is an inspiring story.

It was a very exciting time to be involved: I used my car for transportation jobs and running errands; I helped with the decorating of the houses; I befriended the boys who would be moving in, and eventually helped them settle in. My father, who is an electrician, completely re-wired one of the houses. I was very touched when the trustees of 'Caring for Life' told me that they had decided to call it 'Tindall House'.

Thus began an association with a pastor and people that was to be a source of strength and hope during the months ahead. When I was with Nick and his friends, I was filled with false hopes; I was euphoric from the promise of healing and on a 'high' from their optimism, but as the relationship soured, they left me bereft of hope. God led me to people who spoke to me of Jesus, of his great love for me and of his purpose for my life. They spoke to me of my inheritance that starts on this earth and of its consummation when I enter heaven and see his lovely face. Furthermore they helped me to see that I could work for God now; that my life was not over, but during the remaining time I could live and speak for him, and this I wanted to do more than anything.

Moving On

Peter and I started to meet together during the week for times of fellowship over the study of the Word; however Peter continually emphasised the necessity for me to read and study the Scriptures for myself. He urged me not to accept blindly what he or anyone else said, but always to go to the Bible and test what I had heard. He assured me that the Holy Spirit himself would guide me and help me to understand Scripture rightly and I had already experienced how willingly the Holy Spirit comes alongside us to lead us into paths of wisdom and righteousness.

He suggested I read some of C.H. Spurgeon's sermons which I came to love dearly. One day he gave me a beautiful new copy of Spurgeon's *Treasury of David*. I was overcome by this gesture and have valued the book ever since, both as a gift from my pastor and for its contents, for it represents some of the most wonderful expositions of the Psalms; on many occasions have I turned to the Psalms in great need and found help and comfort there, for the Psalms speak about every joy, suffering and anguish to be found in human experience and in a person's walk with his God.

I was eager to know Peter's views on the subject of healing. It is such a dark, unknown area for me and inevitably,
I had many questions: Why me? For what purpose? What
about the 'promises' I had been told were mine? Promises
such as:
'The days of our lives are seventy years' (Psalm 90: 10);
'Ask, and it will be given to you' (Matt 7:7);
'If two of you agree on earth concerning anything that they
ask, it will be done for them by my Father in heaven.' (Matt
18:19);
'Is anyone among you sick? Let him call for the elders of
the church, and let them pray over him, anointing him with
oil in the name of the Lord. And the prayer of faith will save
the sick, and the Lord will raise him up.' (James 5:14-15.)
These seemed unequivocal promises to me, and I needed
some answers!

Following on from Peter's sermon on 2 Corinthians
12:11-12, I asked him if he thought there were men in the
church today who could perform miracles in the way the
apostles could. We looked at the purpose of the miracles of
Jesus, and in the early church, and decided that they were
there for a reason: namely to verify the truth that was being
preached and for proof of the fact that the men who were
preaching were indeed the mouthpieces of God in a unique
way. Despite some claims by men today, there are no longer
apostles in the church today in the same way that there
were apostles then. Furthermore many 'healings' performed today are incomplete, inadequate and fallacious,
and frequently fail to bring glory to God and vindicate his
word. The healings performed by Jesus and the apostles
were radical and complete: to prove that Jesus was who he
said he was—the Son of God. And even then people did
not believe him. The role of healing in the church today
seems to depend upon emotional settings and psychologi-

cal responses which may result in sad, disappointed people or deluded believers.

We discussed endlessly the possible reasons God might have for not healing me. None of us can see the way ahead and yet we know that God's way is perfect. If God chooses not to heal me, it is not because he is being mean; on the contrary it is because he is being merciful, for he has something better for me ahead. God knows what the most perfect thing would be for me and, indeed, for each of his children. I may never understand it on earth but in heaven I shall fully comprehend and know that God has taken me at the best time for me and the best time for himself. When I am taken to be with him it will obviously be the ultimate benefit and blessing for me—the best thing that can ever happen. And yet while we take no pleasure in the thought of death—the human grief at such a loss is immeasurable— we realised that one of the reasons people today place such an emphasis on healing is because they do not take as seriously as they should the reality of heaven and eternal life.

However, we joyfully affirmed our faith in the God of miracles for we know that 'with God nothing is impossible'. Peter expressed his hope and desire that I should be healed: we knew our God could still heal me, should he choose to do so, but we were content to rest in the promises of God, and desired only that his will be done:

> 'Therefore we do not lose heart. Even though our outward man is perishing, yet the inward man is being renewed day by day. For our light affliction, which is but for a moment, is working for us a far more exceeding and eternal weight of glory, while we do not look at the things which are seen, but at the things which are not seen. For the things which are

seen are temporary, but the things which are not seen
are eternal.   (2Cor 4:16-18.)

A lot of misconceptions had to be stripped away before
the doctrines of grace took hold of my soul. Peter and I discussed theology for hours; I listened to tapes, sermons and
read books, and was able to retain a lot of what I read and
heard. The Holy Spirit had already been my teacher for the
many months I was on my own and my new Christian
friends at L.R.B.C. were able to build on that knowledge.
It was thrilling to meet with other Christians who shared the
same point of view, the same interpretations and above all
could deepen my faith and knowledge of the Lord and of
his Word, for I was ready now for the solid meat of the Word
which is utterly satisfying:

Anyone who partakes only of milk is unskilled in the
word of righteousness, for he is still a babe. But solid
food belongs to those who are of full age, that is,
those who by reason of use have their senses
exercised to discern both good and evil.
(Heb 5:13-14.)

In the sixth chapter of Hebrews, the writer speaks of leaving the elementary teachings about Christ, and urges us to
'go on unto perfection'. What is this perfection? Some
Christians maintain that they are already without blemish:
we know from within ourselves this can never be true;
besides we have chapter seven of the epistle to the Romans
which testifies to the Apostle Paul's continuing struggle with
sin and his 'body of death'. I do believe the writer here is
urging us to overcome our sinful desires, to 'put to death
the misdeeds of the body', and to become more like Christ.
However, this verse also speaks to me of my eternal home,
'the saint's everlasting rest', for 'when one turns to the Lord,

the veil is taken away. But we all, with unveiled face, beholding as in a mirror the glory of the Lord, are being transformed into the same image from glory to glory, just as by the Spirit of the Lord' (2Cor 3:16,18); and 'if [we are] children, then heirs—heirs of God and joint heirs with Christ, if indeed we suffer with him, that we may also be glorified together.' (Rom 8:17.)

Heaven

Many were the nights Peter and I would sit up into the early hours talking about our favourite subject, heaven. It is the main pre-occupation of my thoughts now as I face eternity.

Once we started talking about hell; we discussed various notions of hell including that of a place where people who loved each other in this life would hate and destroy each other in the next. How peculiarly inventive humans are in describing their particular hells, but of course, the real issue is that it is a place where we are cut off from God for ever. In this world the providence of God is seen all around every creature; not one hair falls from our heads nor one sparrow to the ground without the providence of God. As Paul writes in the letter to the Romans: 'For since the creation of the world his [God's] invisible attributes are clearly seen, being understood by the things that are made, even his eternal power and Godhead, so that they [men] are without excuse'. Generally, men do not acknowledge this common grace and are given up to their own desires. Imagine then an eternity where the protecting and sustaining providence of God is removed. It seemed the darkest place imaginable to us that night and soon we could not talk about it any more. The conviction came to us with ever more force that the gospel must be preached to every creature; that our main desire must be to see souls saved by the Holy Spirit. I beg preachers to speak to their congregations about hell only with tears on their faces and sorrow in their hearts. We need our preachers to give us more glimpses of heaven in these days.

In our Bible studies we have looked at the many Scriptures concerning the nature of heaven. We contemplated what it is going to be like there from our consideration of the risen Lord Jesus. People could talk to him, walk with him and touch him; he was neither a phantom nor a ghost but a real human being with a human body that could eat, drink and walk with his friends, and yet as Paul describes it in 1 Corinthians 15, he had a truly spiritual body. We too shall have spiritual bodies, where we shall enjoy doing things together, for we shall be with our brothers and sisters in Christ. Heaven is a place of activity; together we shall explore the new earth and the new heaven and the greatest joy of all will be to be with Christ; we shall see him face to face and like the bewildered disciples of old, we shall be able to touch him, converse with him and worship him through all eternity, for:

> they shall be his people, and God himself will be with
> them and be their God. And God will wipe away
> every tear from their eyes; there shall be no more
> death, nor sorrow, nor crying; and there shall be no
> more pain, for the former things have passed away.
> (Rev 21:3-4.)

Imagine the glory of Jesus; the Bible tells us about the resurrection body of Jesus: we shall be able to walk with him as the two did on the Emmaus road and shall not 'our hearts burn within us' as we converse with him? We shall be able to touch him and press his pierced hands; the crucified Christ is glorified in heaven in a way he was never glorified whilst in our fallen world. When I consider that Jesus left the glory of heaven to come to our world, which is full of misery, sadness, injustice and cruelty, to die for us and save us from our sins, I cannot take it in. He 'did not consider it robbery to be equal with God, but made himself of no reputation, taking the form of a servant, and coming in the likeness of men'. (Phil 2:6-7.) How Jesus must have suffered to leave his home with the Father. Maybe we can understand the full meaning of the transfiguration a little better if we consider it from his perspective. Towards the end of his life here on earth, he was granted a glimpse, a reminder of his heavenly home. What was the effect? 'His face shone like the sun, and his clothes became white as the light.' And I, who want heaven so much; I, who can never imagine leaving it once I have got there, cannot comprehend that my Lord was ever willing to leave it—for me.

To look at Jesus; that is my only thought now. I sometimes shut my eyes and put my head back and imagine what it will be like to see my Lord. To see him coming towards me, to walk arm in arm with Jesus along the golden streets, to converse with the saints...'O that will be glory for me.' The prospect fills me with joy unspeakable, and I cannot understand why some Christians are so worldly. I do believe that the more our thoughts are filled with heaven, the less preoccupied with the world we shall be. As Jeremiah Burroughs says in his book, *The Rare Jewel of Christian Contentment:* 'A carnal heart has no contentment but from what he sees before him in this world, but a godly heart has contentment from what he sees laid up for him in the highest heavens.'

We live in an imperfect world, in terms of natural decay, the greed and selfishness of man, and man at war with man. Even the bride of Christ, people who bear the name of Christ, are imperfect and sadly blemished; Christians are a pale reflection of their Lord. The Christian church is split and divided; anarchy rules in many churches up and down the land. I look, too, at my own body and see the fruits of Adam's sin. Disease and sin reign in this world, but when I start to read and think about heaven, such hope fills my whole being. 'O death, where is your sting?' We shall all be perfect then—physically and spiritually whole. No Christian is perfect now; we aim for perfection but we can never reach that goal until we are made a perfect new creation. The process is begun in this life when we are saved but the work is finished in heaven.

We all have to die sometime and, when we die, we have the assurance that our spirits will be surrounded by the love and presence of God. And in a split second, it could in reality be a thousand years, it will be the resurrection and we shall all be changed and raised to be with Christ for ever. Where would you most like to be at the resurrection? I have heard one minister say that he would like to be at Bunhill Fields in London where so many of the godly puritans and their sons are buried: John Owen, John Bunyan and Isaac Watts amongst many others. Such men have helped me in my spiritual pilgrimage, either by their autobiographies, their hymns or their sermons. God has used them to prepare my soul for eternity and I long to meet them in heaven.

None of us knows what heaven will be like but the Bible gives us many pictures of it and we can imagine! If we consider heaven in earthly terms, the physical features will be intensified and glorified: if there is grass in heaven, it will be brighter and greener than here below; everything will be more than we can ever imagine. And the Lord Jesus will surprise us all. My friend, do you think you know him in this life? Do you ever have glimpses of glory in your devotional life now? These will be nothing compared with the glory which Jesus has prepared for you and for me.

> On this mountain the Lord Almighty will prepare
>> a feast of rich food for all peoples,
>> a banquet of aged wine—
>> the best of meats and the finest of wines.
> On this mountain he will destroy
>> the shroud that enfolds all peoples,
>> the sheet that covers all nations;
>> he will swallow up death for ever.
>> (Isaiah 25:6-8.)

10
Contentment

Every year, over the May Day holiday week-end, L.R.B.C. holds a church conference. I had never experienced anything like it! Four days of intensive sermons, seminars and discussions. It is only in retrospect that I realise how much God used it to speak to me. Thom Smith from America and David Kingdon were the speakers and I have listened to the tapes of their sermons again and again.

David Kingdon spoke on the subject of Christian contentment and warmly recommended *The Rare Jewel of Christian Contentment* by Burroughs. What godly truths are contained in that book, truths that I continually apply to myself in order that I might indeed know 'in whatever state I am, to be content.' Mr. Kingdon urged us to cherish this precious thing, contentment, for it is a rare commodity and so few of God's people appear to have it in this restless, avaricious world. So many people ask me why I am not bitter; my reply is that I can see the sovereign hand of God in my illness, that God allowed me to get cancer to bring me to him—there was no other way that I would have become a Christian. For I was so taken up with a worldly life: if I had been healed in the first place, I would have returned to my old ways because I was not truly saved. God knew what he was doing, and despite all the agony and suffering, I look back and can see why he has done it. I praise him all the time: I would certainly praise him if he took away the cancer but I praise him anyway! He has given me so much—salvation, eternal life, everything, and he has given me time to prepare my soul for eternity. What a privilege! Each day now is an extra bonus: God gives me each new day as a gift and I continually thank him for his blessings to me which are new every morning.

I have never been so contented as I am now. This statement comes as a surprise to many people who assume I should be bitter. How is it possible for a young man of twenty-one years to face agonies of pain relieved only by increased doses of morphine and heroin, the prospect of decreased mobility and, indeed, of death itself, and yet to say that he is happier and more fulfilled than he has ever been? Such is the goodness of God that he has enabled me to learn to be content whatever the circumstances, for 'I can do all things through Christ who strengthens me.' (Phil 4:11-13).

Inevitably there are conflicts still within me: sometimes I just break down and cry. When I see children running and jumping around, when I see images on the television of young people my age, lithe and active, I long to be able to go back in time and to do all those things that once I took for granted. I know what it is like to be disabled and sometimes you feel the world flaunts its agility and vitality at you. If only people could know, for one day, what it is like to be in constant pain and with restricted movement. And then I think of what Christ suffered on the cross for my sins, and I realise that he knows, he understands, he has travelled this

to die in defence of the Bible

path before and he empathises with our suffering and feelings of frustration. It is a great comfort. I wish that I had
become a Christian many years ago and could live a life on
fire for God for many years to come. I lament the wasted

years and wish that I might be granted more time to work and live for him.

It is at such times, especially after I have read accounts in Foxe's 'Book of Martyrs' of how saints died for their faith that I passionately long to lay down my life in defence of the Bible, for the very word of God. I believe all Christians should have this desire and yet I see very little of this. How frustrated I then feel when I consider that I have to die of a stupid disease when I would willingly die for my faith in Christ. And then Jesus comes to me and reminds me that whatever I do, I do it 'as unto the Lord' and he will be glorified in my death as well as in my life.

This, all this, my friends, is Christian contentment and I have only just started to comprehend it! If only we all knew more of our Lord's attitude as we walk through this dissatisfied world so that we might be lights in a dark world, as the apostle Paul says:

Do all things without murmuring and disputing, that you may become blameless and harmless, children of God without fault in the midst of a crooked and perverse generation, among whom you shine as lights in the world, holding fast the word of life. (Phil 2:14-16.)

I have never been so contented

The Heart Of The Matter 11

The tumour was continuing to grow and in June 1987 enquiries were made at the Queen Elizabeth Hospital in Birmingham about the possibilities of a radical 'hind-quarter' operation to remove a large part of my pelvis and the whole of my left leg. St. James's Hospital would not consider undertaking it. Psychologically it was a very hard concept to contemplate: I could not imagine the pain of the operation as the diseased part of my body was removed. I could not imagine re-building my life in terms of the massive disability immediately forced upon me. But it was the last, terrifying resort. The doctors told me that I had already exceeded their prognosis for me and that this was the only option left.

My father took me down to Birmingham for the initial bone biopsy to see if I was a suitable candidate for the operation. I was very apprehensive about it but the staff were very kind and reassuring. The bone biopsy was painful enough and I was unfit to travel back for a few days so I stayed with some former members of L.R.B.C., Gordon and Vivienne Wood. It was while sharing my past experiences with them that we decided to record some of my thoughts and recollections to produce an ordered account of events. People had often said to me that I ought to write a book about the Lord's dealings with me and slowly the vision grew of a book that might bring hope to my family, my friends, and, who knows, maybe to an even wider audience.

Tony with Gordon and Vivienne Wood

I returned to Leeds to await the results from Birmingham. They were a very tense ten days. Finally, Dr. Cartwright from Cookridge telephoned the Birmingham team to find out whether surgical removal was possible. It wasn't. I suppose my worst fears were realised. Even though the operation offered a horrifying alternative, at least it was an alternative carrying hope: now even that was gone. The doctors said that the tumour needed more radiotherapy before they would operate: at the present time it was too advanced. It was not an outright refusal but when I saw Dr. Cartwright she explained that I had already been given the maximum radiotherapy dosage. Although she could not

completely eradicate the tumour, she offered me pain re-
lieving radiotherapy to "quieten it down". Once again we
saw our hopes dashed and I had to adjust to my condition
yet again.

More talks with Christian friends and my precious daily
walk with the Lord helped me to regain my composure. I
began to sense the urgency of the situation; increasingly I
felt that I did not want to talk about trivial things with people.
Peter understood this and our conversations were taken up
for hours and hours with spiritual things. He too wished for
nothing better than to talk about Jesus. I wanted to spend
as much time as possible getting to know the Bible, learning about the truth, and getting to know God. We did a
series of Bible studies together. Peter gave me notes and I
used to go home and study them, covering subjects such as
the nature and revelation of God; the divinity and nature of
Christ—the God-man; what is a Christian? what is the
Bible? how do you study it? I prepared Bible studies myself,
starting with Ephesians 1. This chapter came to mean a
great deal to me as I grappled with those wonderful doctrines of the sovereignty of God: of election, predestination,
sanctification, salvation and glorification and all the other
truths to be found in that single chapter.

Through a right understanding of the sovereignty of God
I can accept that it is far better to be with Christ, but how
do I ever come to terms with the fact that I desperately long
to work for God, here and now, on this earth? It is a frustration that I have never entirely resolved. I long to give
something back to the God who has given me so much. I
long to spend the rest of my days telling others about the
Lord Jesus Christ. However, I am learning to be content
with whatever God allows me to do and I derive a comfort
in writing this book, knowing that this is all I can do now,

but how I pray it will be used as a means of sharing the good news of Jesus with many. I could be a lot worse: if I were worse I would not be able to write this book. God has given me strength to persevere with my testimony of the goodness of God to an unworthy sinner.

God's Provision

Ever since the L.R.B.C. conference, Peter had talked about the possibility of a trip to America to stay with Thom Smith who had become so dear to the fellowship in Leeds during the four days he had spent with us. His ministry had helped many, many people and the tapes of his messages had been sent all around the country to various friends of the church. It never occurred to me that Peter was thinking of including me in the trip! It seemed beyond my wildest dreams when he mentioned it one day. A boyhood ambition of mine had always been that I might get 'jet-lag' and with our proposed lightning tour in July it seemed that that dream might soon be realised!

The providence of God was very much in evidence as we planned the trip: I was kept well enough to travel, God's people gave gifts of money to cover our fares, and even at the last minute, problems with visas and insurance were all covered. They arrived the very day before we were due to fly! We needed to obtain a special licence to take all my medication into America; the authorities were incredulous about my maintenance doses of heroin! The visit was a marvellous experience even though at times I felt rough. It was good to renew fellowship with Thom and to meet his family; I have many memories of the spectacular mountain scenery around Charleston, South Carolina, the fast life in the cities and the friendliness and hospitality of the people. It is an entirely different way of life out there and both Peter and I loved it. The Christians in Thom's church were very welcoming and swarmed around us, relishing our English accents and asking us about our English culture and heritage. Peter spoke at their mid-week meeting, where they welcomed him warmly and were challenged to hear how the Lord had given the vision for 'Caring for Life' and had brought it into being.

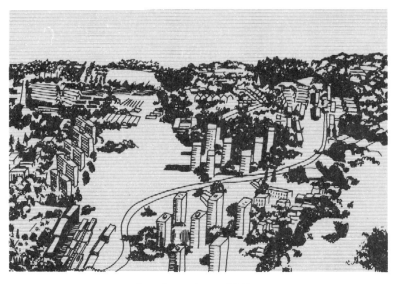

a boyhood ambition

We were in America for just four days; I certainly experienced jet-lag! We returned to a grey English summer which continued for most of July and August. However that

memories of the scenery

weather was better for me; any hot weather had become a burden, for in the heat I became intolerably weak and lethargic. I treasured my independence and the weeks when I felt better I could be seen driving about Leeds, visiting and encouraging church members, and having times of sweet fellowship at the farm in Cookridge where Peter and his family live. I could still go to church and at times my parents came with me.

In September 1987 I became extremely ill. The Macmillan nurse and the district nurse came in every day and they thought I was sinking fast. I had been having trouble with my digestive system and bowels for a couple of months and they assumed I was near the end. They knew that I always wanted the truth and well-meaningly they told us that I had two weeks to live. I have defied all their predictions!

However, at the beginning of October, I noticed an irritation underneath my skin, on my back; we thought it might be a boil, but it turned out to be the tumour breaking through the surface of my skin. Obviously the wound has to be dressed every day and the nursing sisters have been wonderful to me and my family. My mother was given compassionate leave from her work as a beauty consultant in July, and has continued to look after me since then. After being told that I had two weeks left to live, my father stayed at home with me. The support of my family has been immeasurable. I could not have asked for anything more. The way my mother has maintained her cheerful, positive attitude to life has inspired me to fight all the way and she always manages to be welcoming to the scores of visitors that pass through our house. She never gives up hope and I love her for that.

I feel sick all the time now and cannot eat very much. The pain is the worst thing of all. On good days my father will take me up to the farm, but mostly I stay at home, still managing to go on daily walks around Woodlesford. It is eight weeks since I last went to church, but a lot of friends write to me which is a great comfort. Every morning my mother and I have the same routine of opening and reading all the letters that come through the door, some of them from complete strangers who read an article about me in the *Yorkshire Evening Post* and have kept in touch ever since. There are times when I feel very depressed and I do not want to see anybody but mostly I am pleased when friends come to visit me. Above all I take pleasure these days, in reading the Bible and in prayer to God. How thankful I am that I am not too ill to pray. And I can still have Christian fellowship; when I feel well I like nothing better than friends coming and talking to me about the Lord.

One Faith—One Baptism 13

There is one body and one Spirit, just as you were
called in one hope of your calling; one Lord, one faith,
one baptism; one God and Father of all, who is above
all, and through all, and in you all.   (Eph 4:4-5.)

I had been studying the book of Ephesians for some
weeks and when I reached this verse the words struck me
most forcibly. They compelled me to think once again about
the subject of baptism. I had considered it before but now
I felt that the Lord was speaking directly to me, urging me
to follow him through the waters of baptism. I applied to
the elders of the church who interviewed me and spoke to
me about the meaning of baptism and church membership.
They arranged for me to be baptized in my own home on
Wednesday, 28th October. Obviously I could not be baptized by immersion; I would instead be baptized by effu-
sion—by the sprinkling of water upon my face.

It was a very wonderful evening for me, my family and
all the friends who came to witness my testimony. Peter

preached on Romans 8:28-30, some of my favourite verses:

> And we know that all things work together for good
> to those who love God, to those who are the called
> according to his purpose. For whom he foreknew, he
> also predestined to be conformed to the image of his
> Son, that he might be the firstborn among many
> brothers. Moreover whom he predestined, these he
> also called, whom he called, these he also justified;
> whom he justified, these he also glorified.

He spoke about the significance of the words predestined, called, justified and glorified and said that they are all in the past tense. Our predestination took place before eternity began; we know we are predestined when we believe and are justified—it is just as if we had never sinned. Our glorification is also in the past tense for it is certain and secure and procured for us the day Christ overcame the forces of darkness and death itself.

I shared with everybody present what God means to me. I told them that if it were not for my faith I could not go on another day. At times everything seems against me, but I am given strength day by day to carry on. The thought that I will be with the Lord when it is all over gives me such hope for the future. I desired to obey my Lord in baptism, as he told us to do, and to become a member of his body, the church, here on earth. I consider that child-baptism can never make a person a Christian: only when he truly repents of his sins and believes in the Lord Jesus Christ can a person be called a Christian and then he should be baptized.

I was then baptised and the elders welcomed me into the membership of L.R.B.C. After singing my favourite chorus: 'Make me a channel of your peace', we shared the Lord's Supper and all joined together in singing 'Seek ye first the kingdom of God'. Both these songs I would like to have at my funeral.

14 Memories

Two recent events have filled my thoughts with happy recollections as I constantly struggle with the overwhelming
pain. On the evening of Friday, November 6th, my father
took me to Peter's farm for a bonfire and fireworks with the
family. We drove up the long, winding farm track in the
dense blackness of the crisp November night. It was so cold
I was beginning to wish I had stayed at home and the drive
was very uncomfortable. When we arrived, the place was
in total darkness, but as I got out of the car, it seemed as if
a myriad faces surrounded me—beaming, welcoming faces
that burst into song:

> Seek ye first the kingdom of God
> And his righteousness;
> And all these things shall be added unto you,
> Hallelujah…

I shall never forget the experience—there was so much
love surrounding me that night. There was a huge pig roast-
ing on a spit which the boys from 'Caring for Life' had been
turning all day. Peter thrust a lighted torch into my hand

and asked me to light the bonfire. It leapt into flame and by the crackling, glowing light and warmth of the fire, I was able to converse with friends I had not seen for many weeks. The quality of such friendships and memories sustain me day by day in my relentless battle against pain.

The doctors have tried an epidural to overcome the pain but I am constantly in agony. The tumour has come through even more now and I find it impossible to sit down. But as a family we are closer than ever. My mother is a marvellous nurse: she knows every tablet I take, she knows exactly what purpose it serves and keeps the doctors and nurses informed of my needs. My father returned to work but is kept fully involved all the time. We have all encouraged my sister, Louise, to try to live a normal life, so she goes out with her friends most evenings in an effort to cope with the unusual situation at home. Underneath her heart is breaking too. Soon after, my family asked me if there was something I would dearly love to do. I gave it some thought and then told them how much I would love to fly in an aeroplane, to look at Leeds from the sky—not daring to believe that they would manage to arrange it! My mother contacted Anne Pickles, the reporter at the *Yorkshire Evening Post* who had written the article about me, and she told my mother to leave it with her. Within the next few days she had arranged for us all to go up to Yeadon airport for a personal flight in a small, six-seater light aeroplane.

November 11th arrived and we were dismayed to see how foggy and wet it was. We continued to make preparations for the trip even though we assumed that the conditions were too poor for flying. We were about to go when a large blue car slid past our house, turned left into the next road, did a 'U' turn and purred to a halt outside our house. It was a 'Spirit'—a beautiful Rolls-Royce—waiting to carry

Dad, Tony, Mum, Louise

us up to the airport. My mother was overcome as she watched the incredulity and amazement on my face. She had secretly arranged this with a friend of hers. It was the most marvellous experience gliding in this car with its soft white leather interior and its gleaming chrome. I have never experienced such a smooth journey—for a short time we felt like royalty. We rolled up to the entrance of Yeadon airport and the V.I.P. treatment continued; we were warmly welcomed by the airport personnel who did everything they could to give us a very special day.

One of the most remarkable features of the day was the fact that as soon as we arrived at Yeadon, the skies cleared and the sun came out. We were all overwhelmed by the goodness of God for we had all been praying for such a break in the weather. The flight was remarkable; I sat with the pilot in the cockpit and at one point he allowed me to take the controls. The feeling of freedom was superb and I was delighted to be able to identify all the landmarks in the area where I was born and grew up. We took a lot of aerial photographs of our house and neighbourhood which we could see so clearly.

When we returned to ground we were shown around the airport. I was not able to climb the steps to the control tower but I was taken for a ride in a new fire-engine and shown how to use all the latest fire-fighting equipment. I took great delight in pressing a button and releasing 500 gallons of water! Everyone was so kind and it was truly a memorable day. The *Yorkshire Evening Post* included an article on it the following evening.

St. Gemma's Hospice 15

In December the pain became intolerable. I could bear it no longer: neither could I fight it any more. I felt completely overwhelmed. It seemed inevitable that I would have to go into a hospice, which was something I dreaded, for I feared that if I went into such a place, I would never come out again. Such fears and misconceptions proved completely unfounded.

The doctors insisted that I go into St. Gemma's Hospice for at least a week, for them to regulate my pain control. Contrary to my expectations, I found it to be a serene and hopeful place; the Hospice is set in its own grounds and there is a feeling of space and beauty everywhere. I was given a modern room of my own where I could have visitors from 1 p.m. to 11 p.m. In certain circumstances visiting is allowed around the clock and relatives may even sleep there if necessary. Nothing was too much trouble for the staff; they seemed to want to do anything and everything for the patient and his family. The meals were attractively presented and most appetizing. I could not have believed that I would be so comfortable. However, as I started to relax in St. Gemma's, I gradually became aware of more aches and pains all over my body: shoulders, elbows, legs, feet, and buttocks. Nevertheless I was determined to go home on the Saturday as they had promised.

But I was back again the following day. I had been in so much pain at home that my father had to sit with me through the whole night. When we called the doctor from the Hospice, he said that they had not yet begun to tackle the pain and that I would have to return in order for them to build up the pain control.

I returned for two more weeks during which time they adjusted the level of my pain control considerably. For example, before I went into the Hospice I was taking 150 mg of diamorphine (heroin) daily: I now take 1000 mg orally, daily. Similarly they introduced more diamorphine subcutaneously through a 'syringe-driver' so that every 12 hours, another 2000 mg of diamorphine is fed into my body.

The staff at the Hospice were marvellous; they were all so kind and loving. Even after I came home they would 'phone regularly and assure me that my room was waiting for me should I need it. December 17th was my mother's birthday, and the nurses bought a bouquet of flowers for me to present to her. Mum provide a delicious spread of party food and brought a huge birthday cake into my room where we celebrated her birthday in style.

Very reluctantly the medical staff allowed me home the Tuesday before Christmas. The doctors and nurses thought we would never cope at home but my mother and father are formidable. I so longed to be with my family at home— all the time, especially for Christmas, that my parents were determined to manage. However we appeared to have brought half of St. Gemma's with us: pillows, chairs, cushions and sheets... and the Hospice continues to provide a caring and reliable back-up service in a multitude of ways. The doctor comes out at any time, day or night if we need him, and he keeps in touch regularly by telephone. My father has taken leave of absence from work once again as I become increasingly disabled.

Christmas Day was a great success! I felt well and we had a happy day together with other members of our family. We exchanged gifts—something we never dared to believe would happen. Neither did I think I would reach my twenty-first birthday.

Love Never Ends

I was twenty-one on January 2nd 1988! Cars were parked down the length of the street, round the corner and up the other side. I had 51 cards and as many guests dropping in throughout the day. It was an outstanding day—so much love...

It started with the usual routine of the district nurses arriving in the morning, and from then on, the visitors never stopped. Mum once again provided a wonderful spread of food which was steadily devoured as the day progressed. Faithful visitors arrived, and a steady stream of friends and relatives including Peter and Russell, the assistant Pastor at L.R.B.C. The entire district nursing team popped in to celebrate my coming of age with us. They have become real friends of the family and I cannot thank them enough for everything they have done for me. I know at times I have not been the easiest of patients but I love them all and know that I could not be in better hands.

Perhaps the greatest joy and surprise was to renew fellowship with Thom Smith from America, who flew in to

Gatwick that very day for preaching engagements in England, and came straight to see me. I was overwhelmed by all such tokens of love.

To have the pain under control has helped me through; it would have been unthinkable to have enjoyed such an occasion before I went into the Hospice. The present situation is that although the pain is under control, it still seems to be worse at night. I regularly lie awake at night until two or three in the morning (despite 60mg of sleeping tablets!) and it is then that my father plays tapes of sermons or soothing Christian music to me. Many are the nights I lie, wide-eyed with my own thoughts, listening to familiar, well-loved sermons of Peter, Thom Smith and David Kingdon well into the early hours of the morning. Most nights my dear father stays with me until 2 a.m. and I can hardly bear to let him go. These are precious times indeed as he reads a passage from Spurgeon's Morning and Evening, a book that has come to mean a great deal to us both. Then he will read to me from the Bible; we are going through Matthew's gospel at the present time.

I now require help with everything I do because I am losing the use of my legs and have to be carried everywhere. The Macmillan nurse has provided us with an ambulance chair which has greatly eased the problem of going up and down the stairs. The day starts at noon when a district nurse comes in to wash and dress me. My mother and father carry me downstairs where I sit in a chair for the rest of the day. The disease is spreading to my shoulders, elbow and left leg and my feet are very swollen. I dreaded the thought of having a catheter but now it is working so well I wish I had had it earlier as everyone had advised. It is certainly a lot easier for my parents. Twice a week a night-nurse stays with me;

she usually reads Romans 8 to me—this must be my favourite passage from Scripture.

Thom Smith returned to the States last week and came
to say goodbye before he left. It was a profoundly moving
occasion; we talked first and then he read Romans 8 to me.
Fighting back the tears, he prayed with me and said how
much he loved me and had been so glad to have met me.
We were all weeping as he went for he makes an impression wherever he goes. I too have been enriched by knowing him, and by his warm friendship in the Lord.

Blest be the tie that binds
Our hearts in christian love;
The fellowship of kindred minds
Is like to that above.

One of the most important things for me now is that the
reality of heaven should be ever present in my mind especially as I become more poorly. I know that when I lose sight
of the Lord and of the place he has prepared for me then I
become depressed and begin to feel out of touch with God.
While I have a clear picture that heaven is there, that Jesus
is waiting for me, that he loves me with an everlasting love
and whatever he has allowed to happen has been because
the plan of my salvation for eternity was predestined before
the foundation of the world, then I remain secure and at
rest in his love.

In heaven we will be able to touch each other, eat, drink,
walk through doors, but all in a beautiful new earth and new
heaven. Lions and lambs will be lying down together, we
shall build our own houses and eat fruit from the vineyards
we have planted, for as the prophet Isaiah stated long ago:

"For behold, I create new heavens and a new earth…
The voice of weeping shall no longer be heard…
Nor the voice of crying.
No more shall an infant from there live but a few days,
Nor an old man who has not fulfilled his days…
They shall build houses and inhabit them;
They shall plant vineyards and eat their fruit…
The wolf and the lamb shall feed together
The lion shall eat straw like the ox…
They shall not hurt nor destroy in all my holy
    mountain"
Says the Lord.   (Isaiah 65:17-25, selective.)

And when I am conscious of my increasing immobility I turn to these verses:

He gives power to the weak,
And to those who have no might he increases strength.
Even the youths shall faint and be weary,
And the young men shall utterly fall,
But those who wait on the Lord shall renew their
    strength;
They shall mount up with wings like eagles,
They shall run and not be weary,
They shall walk and not faint.   (Isaiah 40:29-31.)

I long for the day when I will run and not be weary, walk and not faint, and indeed, mount up with wings like an eagle, for most surely I will do these things soon.

I have been giving a lot of thought to the verses with which I should close. About a year ago, every day before my mother went to work, I used to choose a verse from the Bible for her and write it down as 'A thought for the day'. She still has sheaves of these verses and we were looking through them the other day to find my favourite verses. I should like to close with 1 Corinthians 13:4-12, for I have known so much love, firstly from my dear mother, father and sister, who have supported me devotedly throughout my illness, (as Bob Johns said they would—it seems a long time ago now), and then from all my friends, neighbours, doctors and nurses. Above all, I have known the love of God in Christ Jesus and if you substitute 'Jesus' for 'love' in the following verses, you will learn that these attributes are only perfectly fulfilled by him:

> Love is patient, love is kind. It does not envy, it does not boast, it is not proud. It is not rude, it is not self-seeking, it is not easily angered, it keeps no record of wrongs. Love does not delight in evil but rejoices with the truth. It always protects, always trusts, always hopes, always perseveres. Love never fails... Now we see but a poor reflection; then we shall see face to face. Now I know in part; then I shall know fully, even as I am fully known. AMEN.

No More Tears

Tony went to be with his Lord at 10 a.m. on Wednesday, 2nd March 1988. His father read these words to him from Spurgeon's *Morning and Evening* the night before he died:

March 1 — Evening

$\qquad$ *He is precious* $\qquad$ 1 Peter 2:7

As all rivers run into the sea, so all delights centre in our Beloved. The glances of His eyes outshine the sun: the beauties of His face are fairer than the choicest flowers: no fragrance is like the breath of His mouth. Gems of the mine, and pearls from the sea, are worthless things when measured by His preciousness. Peter tells us that Jesus is precious, but he did not and could not tell us how precious, nor could any of us compute the value of God's unspeakable gift. Words cannot set forth the preciousness of the Lord Jesus to His people, nor fully tell how essential He is to their satisfaction and happiness…

Dear reader, what would you do in the world without Him, in the midst of its temptations and cares? What would you do in the morning without Him when you wake up and look forward to the day's battle? What would you do at night, when you come home jaded and weary, if there were no door of fellowship between you and Christ? Blessed be His name, He will not suffer us to try our lot without Him, for Jesus never forsakes his own. Yet, let the thought of what life would be without Him enhance His preciousness.

❊   ❊   ❊   ❊   ❊

I am going to my fathers, and though with great difficulty I am got hither, yet now I do not repent me of all the trouble I have been at to arrive where I am. My sword, I give to him that shall succeed me in my pilgrimage, and my courage and skill, to him that can get it. My marks and scars I carry with me, to be a witness for me that I have fought his battles who will now be my rewarder.

(Mr. Valiant-for-Truth, *The Pilgrim's Progress* part II, John Bunyan).